Get Around

on Water

Get Around
on Water

by Lee Sullivan Hill

Carolrhoda Books, Inc./Minneapolis

For Merle and Lois Hill.
—L. S. H.

For more information about the photographs in this book, see the Photo Index on pages 30–32.

The photographs in this book are reproduced through the courtesy of: © Jerry Hennen, cover; © Michele Burgess, pp. 1, 10, 12, 27; © Buddy Mays/Travel Stock, pp. 2, 7, 9, 18, 19, 21, 22, 24, 26, 29; © Robert Fried, p. 5; © Betty Crowell, pp. 6, 8, 13, 14, 15, 16; © Susan Kelm, David F. Clobes Stock Photo, p. 11; Woods Hole Oceanographic Institute, p. 17; © U.S. Navy, PH3 Douglas E. Houser, p. 20; © Portland Rose Festival Association, p. 23; © Bob Firth/Firth Photobank, p. 25; © Sophie Dauwe/Robert Fried Photography, p. 28.

Carolrhoda Books, Inc.
A Division of the Lerner Publishing Group
241 First Avenue North, Minneapolis, MN 55401 U.S.A.

Website address: www.lernerbooks.com

Library of Congress Cataloging-in-Publication Data

Hill, Lee Sullivan, 1958-
    Get around on water / by Lee Sullivan Hill.
      p. cm. — (A get around book)
    Includes index.
    Summary: Describes many of the ways people move themselves
and goods around on rivers, lakes, canals, and oceans.
    ISBN 1-57505-309-8
    1. Navigation—Juvenile literature. 2. Ships—Juvenile literature.
3. Boats and boating—Juvenile literature. [1. Shipping. 2. Boats and
boating. 3. Ships.] I. Title. II. Series: Hill, Lee Sullivan, 1958–
Get around book.
VK15.H45 2000
387—dc21   99-24228

Manufactured in the United States of America
1 2 3 4 5 6 – SP – 05 04 03 02 01 00

Tour boats, rowboats, sailboats, rafts. Many kinds of transportation help people get around on water.

Sailing ships carried people and goods before there were trains, planes, and cars. They traveled on rivers and over seas.

People built canals where rivers didn't flow. Waterways connected places all over the world.

Barges still float along rivers and canals. Large, heavy loads move more easily on water than on land.

Ships carry cargo such as cars and toys, computers and bananas. Cargo ships travel all over the world.

Even small boats help people get around on water.
Farmers paddle to market in town.

Ferryboats carry people along with their cars. Boats can cross water too wide for a bridge.

Water transportation helps many people do their jobs. Fishing boats head out to sea in the early morning light.

Clam fishers work in shallow bays. They unload their
boats at the end of the day.

Dredges work to keep water deep. Dirt and sand wash into the bottoms of rivers. Dredges scoop up the muck so big ships don't get stuck.

Icebreakers keep the way open in winter. Harbors freeze in very cold places. Icebreakers smash a path to open water.

Some boats work to clean up harbors. The pilot aims
the boat at floating trash. A basket in front picks it up.

Other ships take scientists out to sea. Special
equipment helps them study ocean life—from tiny
plants to giant whales.

Some boats are there when people need help. Coast
Guard cutters save people from sinking ships. They
also stop people from breaking the law.

Fireboats come to the rescue when a ship or dock is burning. They pump water from the harbor onto the fire.

The navy protects people with many kinds of ships. Aircraft carriers are huge, like cities on the sea. Navy jets use the top deck as a runway.

Battleships and destroyers are ready if needed to protect their country.

Sometimes water transportation is more than a job—
it's a race! Teams on sailing boats fly across harbors.

Dragon boats use people power to race along rivers.
Everyone wants to win.

There are lots of fun ways to get around on water.
White-water rafts splash down a river.

Water skis skim over a lake. Hold on tight!

Maybe you'd rather take it easy. Paddle a kayak on a quiet lake.

Or cruise to a faraway place.

All over the world, people travel on water. Ships, boats, and rafts help people do work and have fun.

How would you like to get around on water?

Photo Index

Cover The *Delta Queen* is a paddle wheel steamboat that travels up and down the Mississippi River between Saint Paul, Minnesota, and New Orleans, Louisiana.

Page 6 The *Mayflower II* is anchored in Plymouth Bay, Massachusetts. It is a replica, or copy, of the ship that carried the Pilgrims from England to the New World in 1620. Tour guides dressed in clothing from the 1600s show visitors around the ship.

Page 1 Powered by a gasoline engine, this jet ski skims over the ocean near the Hawaiian Island of Oahu. These personal watercraft come in models for one or two riders. They're sort of like snowmobiles for summer.

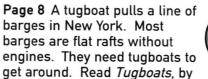

Page 7 This hotel barge motors along the Burgundy Canal in southeastern France. Before engines were invented, mules hitched to towropes pulled barges along canals like this one.

Page 2 This hovercraft carries visitors to the red sand beaches of western Australia. Hovercraft ride on a cushion of air created by giant fans. They glide along above the water and can run right up onto the beach.

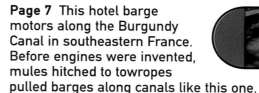

Page 8 A tugboat pulls a line of barges in New York. Most barges are flat rafts without engines. They need tugboats to get around. Read *Tugboats*, by Robert Maass, to learn more about these hardworking boats.

Page 5 A tour boat returns to a marina in Nassau, Bahamas. Various pleasure boats are tied up in slips, which are like parking spaces for boats. Marinas provide electric power and fresh water for boaters.

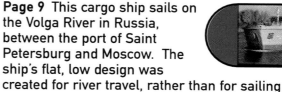

Page 9 This cargo ship sails on the Volga River in Russia, between the port of Saint Petersburg and Moscow. The ship's flat, low design was created for river travel, rather than for sailing on rough ocean waters.

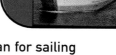

Page 10 These farmers are paddling toward the town of Ywama in the Southeast Asian country of Myanmar. Boats are an especially important form of transportation during the rainy season, when many roads turn into muddy streams.

Page 11 The *Island Queen* travels over Lake Superior between Madeline Island and the city of Bayfield, Wisconsin. A bridge could span the two miles across the lake, but it would be very expensive to build.

Page 12 Fishing, tourism, and agriculture support most residents of rural County Kerry on the west coast of Ireland. This fisher is pulling up his anchor in a cove in Dingle Bay.

Page 13 These clam fishers are unloading their boat in Faro Harbor, Portugal. Clam boats have low sides so fishers can harvest clams from the bay and then easily dump them onto the deck.

Page 14 This dredge scoops up buckets full of sand and dirt from the bottom of the harbor of Santa Barbara, California. Dredges are like big, floating shovels that work to keep water deep.

Page 15 The U.S. Coast Guard icebreaker *Staten Island* is clearing a path into McMurdo Sound in Antarctica. The boat's thick hulls, or sides, make sure that the ice—not the boat—breaks.

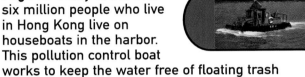

Page 16 Many of the over six million people who live in Hong Kong live on houseboats in the harbor. This pollution control boat works to keep the water free of floating trash and other debris.

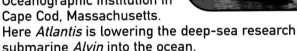

Page 17 The scientific research ship *Atlantis* is operated by the Woods Hole Oceanographic Institution in Cape Cod, Massachusetts. Here *Atlantis* is lowering the deep-sea research submarine *Alvin* into the ocean.

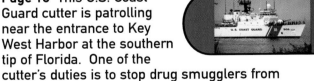

Page 18 This U.S. Coast Guard cutter is patrolling near the entrance to Key West Harbor at the southern tip of Florida. One of the cutter's duties is to stop drug smugglers from entering the United States.

Page 19 Luckily, there is no fire in this picture—the fireboat is on parade, sailing down the Delaware River. Skyscrapers in the city of Philadelphia, Pennsylvania, tower in the background.

Page 20 This photo was taken in 1990, when the U.S. Navy aircraft carrier *Eisenhower* was on duty in the Mediterranean Sea. The jet seen close-up is an S-3A Viking used in antisubmarine warfare.

Page 21 Destroyers and battleships of the U.S. Navy line the docks in Norfolk, Virginia. Norfolk Naval Base is the largest naval base in the United States.

Page 22 The Canadian yacht *Canada II* is racing off the coast of the Caribbean island of Saint Martin. Tourists on the island enjoy watching the exciting yacht races that take place there.

Page 23 Every year during the Rose Festival in Portland, Oregon, colorful dragon boats race along the Willamette River. Each crew of rowers is guided by a captain, who helps the crew row together in rhythm.

Page 24 This family is shooting the rapids in a sturdy raft on the north fork of the Payette River in Idaho.

Page 25 Waterskiing on one ski is called slalom skiing. Beginners learning to slalom find it difficult to balance while a motorboat pulls them up and out of the water, but it's a blast once they learn!

Page 26 These sea kayakers are paddling along Alaska's Inside Passage. Sea kayaks have low sides so strong winds won't blow them around. Space inside the kayak holds supplies, which are protected from water by the closed top.

Page 27 The cruise ship *Island Princess* is sailing along the coast of Alaska in the summer. Wild, remote places such as Glacier Bay, seen here, can be toured from the comfort of the ship.

Page 28 These workers are transporting goods along the Li River in the Guangxi region of southeastern China. Their simple raft is made from bamboo logs tied together with rope.

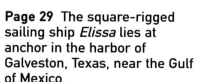

Page 29 The square-rigged sailing ship *Elissa* lies at anchor in the harbor of Galveston, Texas, near the Gulf of Mexico.